Compass Rose

poems by

Heather C. Bryant

Finishing Line Press
Georgetown, Kentucky

Compass Rose

ACKNOWLEDGMENTS

"Mirror" originally appeared in "Lottery Ticket," Heather Corbally Bryant,
The Parallel Press Series of the University of Wisconsin at Madison, 2013.

With thanks to the villages of people who have believed in, encouraged,
read and reread my poetry as I have journeyed from Massachusetts to
Pennsylvania and back home again.

Most of all, thanks to my children who have been the best company on my
journeys, poetic and otherwise.

Editor: Christen Kincaid

Cover Art: Nicholas Benson, www.johnstevensshop.com

Author Photo: Heidi Lynne Photography, heidilynnephotography.com

Cover Design: Elizabeth Maines

Printed in the USA on acid-free paper.
Order online: www.finishinglinepress.com
    also available on amazon.com

Author inquiries and mail orders:
Finishing Line Press
P. O. Box 1626
Georgetown, Kentucky 40324
U. S. A.

Table of Contents

For TBH

September, Hospice

Tamika, I think, might have been her name—on that rainy
September afternoon—she was, I believe, the first person
To say the word death; and after it had been spoken, the

Syllables lived in the room with each of us—my mother,
Terror-stricken, my daughter's eyes strained and wise,
My own heart clenched, shoulders hunched, neck already

Sore at the prospect of what was to come—my mother
Imagined that every breath might be her last, any second
She might go—until her doctor told her, around Yom Kippur,

That she might yet live to see in the New Year—that phrase,
Often repeated, seemed to clear the air, and in the end,

My mother, always obedient, lived thirty days into January.

Horses, Twilight

My daughter used to ride horses—
Hot sticky summers in a barn—
For Christmas a blue velvet
Riding helmet with a bow—

Her father and I fought once
About where on earth to pick
Her up—a hole between us, cracks
In words—we were not together—

Even when we were—at twilight
Now the horses stand on a
Ridge—winter's coming, blankets
Warming, my son and I are driving—

My life is peaceful now,
Westwards, home I can say
Again, what I carry within always.

March Snow, Pine Boughs

The bared circle of ground, a shovel stuck in snow, a mound of dirt—
Suddenly it was all too much for me—I had been thinking of how warm
My mother's body had been as I lay beside her long after she had stopped

Breathing; her fever had been so high her cheeks were still pink, her flesh
Soft as I watched her quilted body being wheeled down the hall to, of all
Things, a minivan, that I had not expected; the undertaker slipped the black

Bag into the back while her nurse stood by to see her patient off to the
Crematorium. She folded the blue quilt silently, then put her arm around
Me as we walked back inside, I could see her cheeks glistening with tears.

Almost two months later, I stood with my children and her friends to bury
The pine box containing her ashes; it had been impossible for me to imagine
How tiny the container would be, how all that my mother had been, and all

That she would be, had been distilled to ash and bone; I never wanted to
Touch her more than at that moment; the minister asked me if I had any
Last words to say and I could not think of a single one; I rushed back to the

Car, skidding on the snowy, muddy ground, and grabbed the letter I had
Written her, the envelope with pictures of her grandchildren, and I reached
Down to place the letter among pine boughs, yellow tulips, rough dirt.

Daylight Savings Time

Optimist that my mother was, at least most of the time, she always
Waited for this season—in fact, she began waiting for it the moment
She saw the days getting shorter—she would say, everyday now,
Everyday, the light will be getting longer; on this first time without her,

We turn the clocks back, it so happened to be that was the day I chose
For her service—she would have loved that, I do know--she would
Have liked nothing better than to see how the light flowed through the
Purple windows of the Memorial Church on that sunny Sunday afternoon

In March, the month of her birth, also by chance St. Patrick's Day—
How I wish I could turn to her and say, "See, the days are getting longer,
Isn't that great?" And I imagine her turning back to me and saying,
"How I wish I were still alive to see the weeping willows greening."

What She Loved

My mom loved tomatoes with their skin peeled; she loved bright colors,
Especially pinks and yellows; she never failed to wear green on
St. Patrick's day, her favorite holiday; she told me socks and
Underwear still counted when I refused to wear the shirt she'd picked
Out for me one year; she loved Rose lipstick from Boots, her favorite
British apothecary; she explained she was wearing that color when
She first glimpsed my dad climbing the basement stairs of the
London embassy; they didn't talk, but each noticed the other.

Though avowedly not religious, she was deeply superstitious; she carried
Several St. Christopher's medals in her change purse; she clutched one
During every Ascent and descent on every trip she ever took; I found one
Still in the green wallet beside her bed; she loved Ireland and spent many
Vacation afternoons there looking for four leaf clovers; she gave me one
She'd found and pressed in saran wrap; on my wedding day, she snuck a
Sixpence in my white high heels; I never knew until I threw them off why
My right big toe hurt so much. She insisted on slipping her wedding ring

Around the candle of every birthday cake, meaning good luck for
Everyone in the year to come; she didn't mind if the flames left singes
Behind; she loved to blow smoke rings; she loved camel cigarettes; she
Smoked a pack a day for twenty years until I told her they made her smell
Bad and I wouldn't sit on her lap; she quit the Day I turned three, and
Never looked back; she wanted to be a diplomat; she loved languages; at
Different points in her life she could speak Chinese, Portuguese, Spanish,
Italian, and French fluently. She always spoke Spanish with her nurse.
She loved to vote; she took me to League of Women Voter meetings; I
Didn't dare tell

Her the one presidential election I skipped; she said I should never turn
Down the opportunity so many women had fought for; she even voted
Absentee for her man, Obama, in the last election; she told me I could
Do anything a man could do and more; she loved education; she gave me
Gold and Lapis earrings when I earned my PhD because she was so proud
Of me; she read every word I wrote, almost.

I learned to wait until I was finished to let her get out her red pen. She
Loved and kept her multitude of friends, many of them dating from her
Teenage years
When she studied abroad in Mexico; then from Swarthmore where she
Ran a Coke

Machine to make extra money; she shared the glass bottles liberally; later,
At Michigan, she loved to play ping pong; there she learned her taste for
Fine scotch; she was an athlete before her time, loving field hockey and
Basketball; she loved tiny packages of Kleenex, and insisted on giving
Me a stash every time I saw her; she loved scarves; she loved pearls and
Emeralds; my father gave her an antique
Emerald surrounded by diamonds when he proposed to her in London.
She loved cities, her native Manhattan, London, then later Boston,
Though she complained it was too provincial, the shopping inferior; she
Loved Bach, Beethoven, Mozart, and

Hayden; she loved Ferragamo shoes because she thought they made her
Ankles look skinny; she loved her collection of ball gowns; she even sent
Me to dancing school because she thought every girl should know how to
Waltz properly; she let me keep her old fancy dresses in my closet so my
Friends and I could play pretend; she
Loved Chanel No. 5, the perfume I now wear to remind me of her. she
Loved books, was always reading several at a time; she loved crossword
Puzzles, finishing the *New York Times* one daily except on Sunday when
She and my dad completed it together;
She loved my dad with all her heart; she loved to listen to him read to her;
Theirs

Was the happiest marriage I have ever known; for forty-one years they
Lived and loved side by side; she once told me she considered herself
The luckiest wife in the world; she loved to write: novels, articles, letters,
Reviews, postcards, birthday cards, notes, lists, always lists; she loved
Grammar. She loved to cook, though not to clean; fortunately, my dad
Loved to wash dishes; that is what they were doing together when she
Went into labor with me ten days early; she loved me more and knew

6

Me better than I ever understood when she was alive; she also loved her
Grandchildren, her descendants, as she used to call them, more than she
Was ever

Able to tell them; she has written her history for them; she showed it to
Me last November and she let me write a bit more she dictated to me.
When I read it, I learned more about her than I had in the fifty-three
Years I was fortunate enough to be her daughter; I am more fortunate
Than I ever knew to have listened—although less than I now wish—to
What she had to say; she loved to tell stories and to laugh; already I miss
Her every day; she loved clouds, their movement, their shape, their form;
When I look up now, I see her there somewhere, telling me what she
Sees—
A horsetail, a whisper, an ice cream cone, a cluster of trees,

A place of peace I know because I was holding her when she let go.

April Third

Thirty-seven degrees on the third day of April—even
Gusts of snow—no one needs to tell us this has been a
Hard winter, that's something we all know by now; I saw two
Purple and yellow crocuses pushing through hard earth,
And a mother leaning down to help her daughter feel
Their soft sprouts, promising her that spring was real.

Planting Pansies, Chicago

Pansies, perhaps, are the most hopeful of plants,
First to be planted, a ritual of spring, even when
It is still sleeting this mid-April Saturday, almost
Tax day—I freeze as I walk against wind-blown

Gusts thrusting against me, pellets of sleet or hail,
I can't be sure which, sharp against my cheeks,
The scene is bleak; it would be easy to become
Sad, as my grandmother must have, pacing these

Streets, wondering where she and her daughter
Would next sleep, or eat, or live—over eighty
Years ago—today, I watch gardeners bundled
Up, planting budding midnight blue, apricot petals.

Bomb

My son texts me, having just landed from Tempe—
"Boston. Bomb," the first I'd heard of a city thrown
Into chaos, fear, limbs thrown everywhere—

Two young men, the same age as my eldest,
Have turned Boston upside down—who knows the
Workings of the human heart, of where they got

Their start on this horrific scheme, a nightmare
Conjured out of a blue sky, a sunny day, chosen
Apparently because so many would be nearby.

Morning, Zurich

The Swiss sun awakens me, coming through the plane's
Shades and I am surprised to have slept almost through
The night, this first trip to Europe by myself in a long time.

I am learning about who I used to be, before, before
Everything that happened, how I used to see the world:
We sleep, we dream, we wake—each day is ours to keep.

Easter, Santorini

Propelled by the crowds, I follow a wave of people
Towards the church square; it is beautiful there—
The blue dome luminescent, rising to the sky

And I see candles blessed and lit, shouts, commotion,
A fight—fireworks everywhere—faces illuminate,
Sparklers tossed in the air, "big bombs coming,"

A grandfather warns, we are all swept along with
Passion arising—a bit fearful, I climb some stairs
To watch the crowd below celebrating the glory and

The resurrection—walking back, I pass Greek lilies
In bloom—gunpowder lingers in the air amidst the
Sweet blossoms, may our world last forever, Amen.

Ancient Thera

How did these ancient people carry such heavy loads
For such long distances, that's what we want to know—

And how did they carve such delicate patterns and
Designs into such thick rocks—how did they balance

A statue of Aphrodite on this rectangular pedestal—
On this spit of land, cliff jutting out into the Mediterranean

Sea—stone carvers must learn, practice, and perfect
Their art, like any other—maybe it should come as no

Surprise that they fashioned these shapes—three days
After our visit to the ruins, the man who is carving my

Mother's stone calls me, just to double check her dates,
Hard to believe she's been gone eight months, that she

Lived almost to the end of her eighth decade—I like to
Remember her story of visiting Greek ruins with my father.

Hiking to Fira

Sunday afternoon, a sultry island day: sunshine pours heavy,
Sweat clings to my forehead, just sitting outside reading
Under a white umbrella makes me perspire; I delay

Packing for my trek to Fira: eventually, I select water,
Camera, sunscreen, a watch but no map, the sign is easy to see—
I cannot possibly miss it on the way out of Oia, or

So Maria says. I start my dusty walk along the switchback road
For at least a mile; early on I spot specks of people crossing
By a church on high, I want to get to where they are. I

Take a sharp right upward turn scrambling uphill where I only see
The remains of a house started, foundation half poured, haphazard
Rocks set in unlikely places. I wonder if I can reach the path from

Here just by digging my feet into the mountain; I hear a voice
Of reason, the trail will be difficult to catch, besides it is very steep
And I am carrying a heavy pack; it will be a long way back.

Dejected, I turn around, and take pictures of the view by a
Scenic lookout as if to say this venture today has not been in vain
After all; not at all, a few turns later I call out aloud when I

Spot a sign, crooked, backwards, mysterious like so much else
In Greece—I decide to give it a try, spending hours climbing
The ridge until I can see both sides of Santorini, as promised;

I pass rocky cliffs, cement chains of houses begun, abandoned
Apparently in haste, resorts with tempting pools, a blue dome
Where I almost make another wrong turn until I glance to

My left and see the white town of Fira rising in the distance
At almost the most beautiful hour just before the famous sunset—
Rose-tinged light splashing on the Mediterranean ocean below.

Mirror

As if still in a dream, I woke thinking of you—
Sometimes I don't believe you are real, here,
My daughter, always—you have a way about

You, something I can't explain, something
Magical, ethereal, as if you came from some-
Where far away from this earth—I remember

You inside me, somersaulting, always moving,
From the beginning you were a mystery; we
Could not see your face—and what a beautiful

Face it is, but a beauty that cannot be described,
Or explained, just the way you are, the way you
Came to me one snowy day in January, blue eyes

Open already squinting at the world—if I had
Only one wish for you—and you know that I
Have many, but perhaps this is the most

Important wish—it is that you learn to look
Inside yourself for strength, love, passion,
Joy, peace, tranquility—it is all already there,

As if waiting for you to turn your gaze
Inward to receive just what you need—
By staring long enough at who you are,

That is how you know who you will be.

The First of June

I always find this time of year filled with poignant
Beauty, a certain fragility of tenderness beginning,

Saplings taking root, girls in white dresses carrying
Red roses walking towards their new lives, boys

Uncharacteristically hugging one another—and I
Remember my own breasts leaking, overflowing

With milk as I leaned down to place the dirt upon
My father's grave, the Chinese dogwoods just having

Come into bloom in those heavy days of early June.

August, Montmartre

Alone, up early to beat the heat, I sip
A steamy cappuccino in a demi-tasse,
Sprinkled with a tube of sugar—my

Son and daughter are still sleeping—
They are teenagers who stumble out
Of bed late—I remember what it was

Like to want to sleep til noon, to think
My parents were weird for waking early—
I watch men and women walk down the

Stairs of the metro beside the carousel,
Still closed, pink and gold horses stilled,
And I think of how my daughter used

To beg to ride them, round and around;
She never got dizzy—now she walks
Tall beside me, to her disgruntlement,

After just one summer away, she has
Become far better at speaking French
Than I ever was, or will ever be—

Biking, Luxembourg Gardens

My friend meets me by the velo stand—
She has mastered the system—we charge
Our cards and remove our bikes—

A Saturday in August, everyone except
The tourists is leaving Paris—the streets
Are empty, just some passing cars, a few trucks—

We bike down the steep hill from Montmartre
Along the boulevards, past the Louvre, beside
The plane trees which give us much necessary

Shade until we end up by the fountains in the
Luxembourg Gardens—we buy cappuccinos
From the small stand by the reflecting pool

Where young boys and girls float their toy boats—
We mostly have the garden to ourselves—
The hot sun begins to rise higher before we

Begin our climb back—she is teaching me how to be,
At any given moment, simply in that one place
And time: early one August morning in Paris.

Listening to Seamus Heaney

I

The first time I heard this man read I thought I was sophisticated,
But really I was so young, a sophomore in college; I sat between my
Mother and my father; I was so busy, almost too busy to meet them
For this occasion. I remember how the words spilled forth that April
Afternoon from Heaney, the first living poet I had heard speak. I
Remember the sounds of his syllables, a poem called "Mint,"
Written after the death of his mother, the aroma of the mint she
Grew in her garden; afterwards, I told my father I wanted to be a poet;
He had been bemused, but my world had changed, I had heard a person
Explain the sorcery between the conception of an idea and a dream,
And how that magic makes a poem; I was too busy, or so I thought,
To take Heaney's course on prosody, too busy to know my own truth.

II.

As a young married woman, I heard him read for the second time
In Sanders Theatre, to a crowd filled November room; he was famous
By then, but still so humble, he explained the origins of one of his poems,
How the idea of procreation had come to him when he had peeked out
His window to see the black bag his mother's doctor
Carried with him every time just before another brother or sister
Arrived; Heaney described how he thought the baby came in
The bag, when he was supposed to be sleeping; I did not have children then,
But yearned for them, longed to be a mother; I listened to how he spoke
As both son and father. I cursed myself for not taking his course when
It was right in front of me, everything there but for the asking.

III.

Of course I read every word he wrote throughout the years, and I thought
Often of how he spoke, reminded once again alone at Harvard on a warm

October evening when the Cambridge fire brigade had to intervene
Because students filled the pathways, blocking the corridors, a hazard
To public safety. The chief fire marshal ordered half the audience
Outside where they went, disgruntled and disobliged, hanging on
The windowsills by their fingertips to hear Heaney's words floating
Through the fall evening; by then I had children, but I was already
Distrusting the contours of my life; I found his poems a comfort.

IV.

Just knowing he inhabited the universe gave me hope; so I stood
Alone in a long line waiting to have "Opened Ground" signed—he looked
Up at me after scribbling his name and said "Good luck," or "Godspeed,
I can't remember which, and I left that room carrying the memory
Of him with me as someone who would always bear the truth of word
And soul; I reread "Mint" in the days following my own mother's
Death and I thought of how words can live forever, but not people,
Just the memory of his voice reading came alive to me; his words
Always with me; the notice of his death that August morning, close
After my own mother's, came as a shock, his voice stilled, impossible.

A Good Rain

A woman says it hasn't rained for eleven days, her parched garden sure could use some water; a man says it's a good rain we need, a rain to last all day, other people complain that they are soaking wet from the sky's opening—I wonder what a bad rain would be, what would we call that—in college it rained for every important event: move-in, move-out, commencement and, finally, of course, for every reunion—I remember walking back late from a party, so late the subway had stopped running, and halfway home we felt the first drops, none of us had the money for a taxi so we laughed about how wet we would get, how we would tell our kids about running from the raindrops at night under the leafy Chestnut trees.
Now my students and I joke that it rains every Thursday, just before our class starts.

Penultimate

Omnipresent, omniscient, omnivore, carnivore, carnival, carnation, words turning over and again in my mind, until my eyes practically go blind, words and words and more words, scampering across the screen, college words, big words, little words, all words, no words, too many feelings, not enough feelings, not enough of the right kinds of feelings, why do some languages have so many words for snow and we are so far from being able to let our true feelings show? Tri, triple, trifecta, triple play, those are always words we say; and I have my favorites like penultimate, second to last, maybe thinking the first shall be last and the last shall be first, maybe because I am always wondering what the world will be like, about what lies on the other side.

Compass Rose

Stella Maris, Star of the Sea

How it came to be carved on my father's grave
I do not know—somehow now it lies among the
Autumn leaves, and the already ripened bright

Red crab apples, fallen now, red against the
Yellow birch leavings—and everything seems to
Be leaving, softly leaving—my mother, my father,

My husband, the house where I grew up—all softly
Leaving—this time last September I keep repeating
Silently, this time last year I was watching my mother's

Mind take leave—she was there, in the flesh, but
She was wandering, meandering, wanting to go away—
Somewhere far away, though she knew not where.

Exactly a year later, I learn that I am coming home
To New England, soil of rocky ledge, home of sea roses
And primroses—I wish I could tell my mother—but

Maybe she knew, as mothers do, that I would be able
To find my way, guided perhaps by the lines etched on
The pink granite gravestone she now shares with

My father—my student tells me the compass rose,
Also known as Windrose or Rose of Winds, dates from
1200 AD, and was the first compass to display the cardinal

Points and their intermediate directions—how to get
From here to there, even when no one else is there—
A Compass Rose was once displayed on the Tower of

The Winds in Athens, so long ago in history—I like to
Believe that's why my father chose that symbol—he
Believed in the power of the atlas—he loved to read maps;

They were a guide for him of a life well-lived, from
West to east, and back again, he picked up the pieces of
His life when his first wife left him—I know, if he could have,

He would have helped me find my way out of my long
Marriage—he would have told me what he had learned,
That even though he did not believe it at the time,

The gate could swing open again, the road could
Stretch out ahead, long, empty, and free—and the
Big wide sky would be there to watch over me.

Somehow I knew to head east, eastward towards
The ocean, towards the shoreline where the water
Meets the land—But first I had to learn the points

Of the compass all over again—I had to open a new
Map and keep it with me even when the first drops
Of rain came, or the soft snowflakes, or the early

Snowdrops sprouted—I had to learn how to feel
At home in my own skin, like a snail, to carry my
House on my back until I could hear the call of the

Sea—my father cautioned me never to turn a map
Upside down to read it—for him, that was a cardinal sin.
So I followed the Stella Maris, the Star of the Sea—

And I knew that, if I followed the direction of this
Compass star I could find my way home and all the
Places that had been familiar would be so once more,

All the shorelines I had known would come back to me—
And it would be better to be alone than to be trying to get
Blood out of a stone—instead, I will embrace what I know,

Where I believe I can go, where I will make my own
Weather, where I will remember where north is,
Where the simple cross marks the ancient path,

Just like in Thera, and I will walk towards the sea,
I will smell a salty ocean, see purple morning glories
Tumbling over stone walls, and I will be walking

East towards the crushed bones of the people who
Made me, and I will make a new home for the
Children I have made and the children they will

Make after them, and then I will keep traveling
Towards home, towards the land where I have always
Wanted to be, where the water rolls over the shore,

Where the low tide recedes, brackish, then rises again.

Heather Corbally Bryant (formerly Heather Bryant Jordan) currently teaches in the Writing Progam at Wellesley College. Previously, she taught at the Pennsylvania State University, the University of Michigan, and Harvard College. She received her A.B. with honors in History and Literature from Harvard where she received the Boston Ruskin Prize for her thesis, *Sight and Sensibility: A Study of Praeterita.* She received her Ph.D in Modern British and Irish Literature from the University of Michigan where she was a Regents Fellow. She has won outstanding teaching awards from Michigan, Harvard, and most recently, from Penn State.

Her academic publications include, *How Will the Heart Endure: Elizabeth Bowen and the Landscape of War,* (University of Michigan Press, 1992). This study of the relationship between war and literature was awarded the Donald R. Murphy Prize for best first book. In addition, she has assisted in the research for the Cornell Yeats Series as well as publishing articles on Bowen, Yeats, O'Faolain, and T.S. Eliot. She has given papers at international conferences and was a plenary speaker at the centennial celebration of Elizabeth Bowen held at University College, Cork, in 1999.

Beyond her academic publications, Heather Corbally Bryant has published a novel, *Through Your Hands* (2011) which received an Editor's Choice and Rising Star designation. Her first poetry chapbook, *Cheap Grace,* was published by Finishing Line Press in 2011. In addition, she has published poems in *The Christian Science Monitor* and the 2007 anthology of poetry, *In Other Words. Lottery Ticket,* was published by the Parallel Press Poetry Series of the University of Wisconsin Press in 2013. She has given readings at The Pennsylvania State University, The University of Wisconsin at Madison, The University of Illinois at Chicago, Southern Florida University in Ft. Lauderdale, Webster's Bookstore, State College, Folio Bookstore in San Francisco and the Palmer Art Museum in State College. *Compass Rose,* her third poetry collection, is forthcoming from Finishing Line Press in February 2016.

www.ingramcontent.com/pod-product-compliance
Lightning Source LLC
LaVergne TN
LVHW091235080426
835509LV00009B/1297